GW01607699

Wembley: 50 Glorious Years in Pictures

Colin Stuart

Wembley: 50 Glorious Years in Pictures

David Bruce & Watson · London

First published in 1971 by
David Bruce & Watson Limited
277-9 Gray's Inn Road, London WC1

ISBN 85127 003 4

Designed by Len Embry

Printed and bound by Hollen Street Press Limited, Slough, Buckinghamshire.

Contents

Introduction

Among soccer fans the world over, Wembley is the greatest, and these are the pictures that record for all time its finest moments. No other stadium anywhere can match the magic of Wembley's glories, past and present. Incredibly, the twin-towered sports complex is about to celebrate its fiftieth birthday. It was created in 1923, as a jewel in the crown of the last great British Empire Exhibition atop a Wembley hill. The first immense labour of its birth was the excavation of 250,000 tons of clay from the crest, where only a local folly and a golf course had stood. The aim of the builders was to create 'the finest sports ground in the world' and that they were far ahead of their time is implicit in the fact that, fifty years later, it still well deserves that title.

But there were few who would give a farthing for its chances of success in the depressed days of the early 'twenties. Where in hell was Wembley anyway? asked the critics. And they answered themselves by chronicling the fact that it was an ugly 'village' which commuters rushed through on the Metropolitan Railway on their way to Harrow-on-the-Hill. Its only mention in the history books was a derisory one, when King Offa valued its 500 acres at 30 shillings in 757 AD.

No-one, the 'knockers' opined, would be bothered to travel the 10 miles from London to visit so undistinguished a place, even if it was to feature the finest exhibition Britain had ever staged.

The Prince of Wales, however, with his 'common touch' gift of knowing the needs and dreams of the man-in-the-street, saw clearly that the sports complex could be the key to the success of the entire project. Speaking at a meeting of Dominions' Prime Ministers in 1921, he urged financial and other help for 'a great national sports ground', which he knew 'would appeal to all Britishers' and which could become the Mecca for world soccer. His speech fanned a flame that had been flickering in the hearts of people starved of the escape offered by the great sporting occasion. Money flowed in. Wembley was on the lips of millions.

Edward quickly followed through on the interest he had created. He called a meeting of Lord Mayors and civic heads from all over the UK and told them: 'A large work of preparation has to be done which will be a cause of immediate employment for thousands of men who have already served their country well — my old comrades, the ex-Servicemen.' The timing and the mood were exactly right. Everyone set-to with such a will that the giant stadium was completed and used triumphantly for soccer a full year before the Empire Exhibition was ready.

Even today the facts and figures about Wembley Stadium are stunning. It is 890 feet long and 650 feet wide. The twin towers, from which the royal standard has so often broken over the years, soar up to 126 feet. To form the 40 miles of terraces, 25,000 tons of concrete were mixed, poured and shovelled in days when concrete mixers were rare. The framework consisted of 1,400 tons of structural steel, together with 600 tons of reinforcing steel and 500,000 rivets. The emerald turf was surrounded by a quarter of a mile of running track — the only one of its kind in Europe. Beneath the stands was room for 1,000 athletes, plus dressing-rooms, showers, buffets, tea-rooms and banqueting halls.

The great new British sports centre, incredibly carved out in 300 working days, from the cutting of the first sod to the adding of the last turnstile, at a cost of only £750,000, was inevitably compared with that wonder of the ancient world, the Colosseum at Rome, with Wembley Stadium winning hands down in measurements and capacity. Nor did Wembley lack support, variety and staying-ability when it came to the bit. The critics were at once proved to be as wrong as it is possible to be. In the first three years of its existence, following the opening event of 1923, when a world-record crowd watched the incredible 'white horse' Cup Final, millions visited the stadium to see cavalcades, rodeos and spectacles of almost every conceivable sort. And thereafter, the changes would be wrung on almost every kind of outdoor sports event, taking in speedway, greyhounds, athletics, Rugby League, boxing, hockey, show-jumping . . . And the adjoining Empire Pool would in due course add tennis, swimming, diving, water-polo, skating, ice shows, cycle-racing, table-tennis, darts, basket-ball and a host of other attractions.

These are the ingredients of the Wembley story. But many though the hats are which the stadium wears in the course of a year, none can match the great soccer occasions.

The Empire Stadium goes from glory to glory as the cliff every international team seeks to climb; as the ultimate chapter-heading in every club player's proposed auto-biography; and as the ultimate excuse for every fan to cheer his team to glory. It's all here, in pictures that freeze the busy ball and capture the joy or anguish of the great occasion; with *all* the memorable Cup Finals plus the greatest names of now and of soccer history. Read it, keep it and treasure it.

The 'white horse' final

This was the scene at the first Wembley Cup Final. It was the afternoon of Saturday, 28 April, 1923. The teams were waiting in the tunnels. The King was in his seat. But three-quarters of the playing area was occupied by fans, for the very good reason that nearly 200,000 people had obtained admittance to a stadium built to hold less than half that number. The turnstiles had mistakenly clicked in 126,047; the other 75,000 had rushed the gates or climbed the fences; and there were still 100,000 outside the stadium, locked out but unable to move away.

The position looked hopeless, and officials were about to call the match off, when up rode P.C. George Storey on his white horse Billie (*ringed in our picture*). A quiet push here; a gentle shove there . . . and gradually a miracle was seen to be happening, as the crowds responded to the mounted policeman. It was a typically English solution and a typically English response. Elsewhere in the world, guns, batons and smoke might have been chosen . . . with deaths, perhaps, the outcome. At Wembley, not one person in the vast crowd was injured and the match was played and enjoyed in great good humour throughout, thanks to a bobby and his faithful steed.

1920's

The 'white horse' final

West Ham attack the Bolton Wanderers' goal, as part of the enormous crowd swans around the posts and presses in on the verges to see the action. It was the first ever Cup Final at Wembley, and the Hammers eventually went down to a brilliant Trotters' side (in white shirts) which featured the great goal-scoring attacker, David Jack, who achieved the honour of scoring the first-ever goal in a Wembley final.

The pomp and circumstances

The great Empire Exhibition, of which Wembley's Empire Stadium was a dazzling part, opened on St George's Day, 23 April 1924, with a State ceremony of suitable magnificence. This was immediately followed by the King and Queen moving among their subjects as though demonstrating that they too could enjoy such a celebration when the occasion called for it. They even visited the amusement park and were pictured enjoying the quieter 'rides'.

This is the famous Wembley Scenic Railway. Prince George puts on a knowing smile for the camera in the cramped front seat beside his mother, the Queen, while a bowler-hatted detective receives an inevitable umbrella from an unseen aide. The sun was shining, but one never knew . . . and no raindrop should be allowed to fall on the flowers in Her Majesty's gay hat.

Can this, too, be Wembley?

Queen Mary's hats were always spectacular — as was the Empire itself on which the sun never set! The most magnificent of our imperial queens towers above her loyal subjects as she inspects the Burmese Pavilion at the Exhibition which showed, for the last time, the greatness of that Empire.

Jack and Jill can look at a queen

Chairoplanes fly overhead as Queen Mary walks among her subjects, protecting her skin from the sun's rays, while the ever-attentive detective marches alongside with the maybe-necessary umbrella and maxi-cloak just in case April showers disturb the serenity of the right-royal occasion.

Left-wing pair

Bolton Wanderers are back at Wembley for the second time in four seasons. King George V, bowler-hatted, with a flower in his buttonhole, shakes hands with Joe Smith, who, in partnership with Ted Vizard, was to show for years what an understanding pair could achieve in combined probing thrusts down the left wing. The Trotters from Bolton, with only one change from the 1923 team, bamboozled their way to victory over a powerful Manchester City Team, by the only goal of the match – scored by David Jack from a pass from Vizard from a pass by Smith . . .

Never at sea

Dick Pym, a Lancashire fisherman turned goalkeeper, who was one of the stars of the 1926 final, is seen here on his knees during a Manchester City attack on the Bolton goal.

First-ever broadcast

This all-ticket crowd – the largest since the extraordinary scenes of 1923 – watches a thrilling match between Cardiff City (dark shirts) and Arsenal, the latter incredibly making their first appearance in a Cup Final since their founding, as Royal Arsenal, in 1886. The attendance was 91,206, and the receipts were £23,113. This 1927 final also made history by being the first ever to be broadcast, with a commentary by George Allison.

The 'foreigners' win at Wembley

Arsenal are seen attacking the Cardiff City goal in the 1927 final. But it was Cardiff who were to make history, in winning by one goal, by becoming the only 'foreign' club ever to win an English Cup Final. Not that it was a Welsh team in terms of players. Cardiff City's line-up featured one Englishman, four Irishmen, three Scots and only three Welshmen. The goal was scored by Hugh Ferguson, the club's Scottish-born centre-forward.

Graf Zeppelin over Wembley

An ominous shadow falls over Wembley Stadium as Arsenal play Huddersfield Town in the 1930 Cup Final. Germany's power-hungry boasts of coming air power have found their shape in the giant Graf Zeppelin airship, which they have sent over to impress the English on their greatest sporting day of the year.

Arsenal the great

A keen soccer fan by now, bearded King George V inspects the Arsenal team before the 1930 final. Managed by the great Herbert Chapman, this was the all-conquering Arsenal side that used the new offside rule to advantage in brilliant offensive raiding. The Gunners lined up as follows: Preedy; Parker, Hapgood; Baker, Seddon, John; Hulme, Jack; Lambert, James and Bastin. The forward line was one of the greatest ever seen at Wembley.

The Herbert Chapman final

Huddersfield Town, previously managed to success by Herbert Chapman, can do little to match the 'third back' game he has introduced to Arsenal in time for the 1930 final. The incomparable 'Wee Alex' James, of the baggy shorts and twinkling feet, beats Turner, the Huddersfield goalie, all the way with this early goal, from a pass from 'Boy' Bastin that was later described by disgruntled Huddersfield fans as 'a conjuring trick'. Lambert scored Arsenal's second goal six minutes from the end of a sizzling final.

Salute to the Cup

Mud-bespattered but proud, West Bromwich Albion captain Glidden embraces the FA Cup, presented to him by the Duke of Gloucester after the 1931 final against Birmingham, as a police officer salutes him and a caped 'bobby' stands to attention.

First leg of a great 'double'

West Bromwich Albion score their first goal against Birmingham City in the 1931 final, as the mainly-Midlands crowd glory in a hard-fought game. WBA, in winning 2-1, made history by being the first-ever second division side to win at Wembley. A week later they deservedly clinched promotion to division one.

All done by numbers

Action around the Manchester City goal in the thrilling 1933 final, in which Everton won convincingly to pull off a remarkable hat-trick – winners in three successive seasons of second division, first division and FA Cup. It was the first final in which the players wore numbered jerseys.

The conquering heroes

The fabled Bill 'Dixie' Dean shows the FA Cup at the train window as the victorious Everton team return home to Liverpool to the cheers of their fans at Euston station, on the Monday after the 1933 final, in which they defeated Manchester City 3 - 0.

Indoor arena

The Empire Pool is added to the Empire Stadium, at Wembley, at a cost of £200,000. Opened by the Duke of Gloucester, using a golden key, in July, 1934, it was the finest indoor arena of its kind anywhere, featuring 300 dressing rooms, 1,500 lockers, seating for 8 – 12,000 spectators, and a roof span of 240 feet, giving an uninterrupted view even from the cheapest seats. Introduced for swimming and diving, it was later to feature skating, ice-hockey, boxing, athletics, professional tennis, table-tennis, darts, plus a host of other indoor sports and entertainments.

Thrills and spills

In early announcements about the possibilities the Empire Pool would open up, Wembley boss, Arthur Elvin, is on record as saying that the only sport he could not foresee there was cycling. He was to eat his words soon after the opening when a banked track was installed to feature the thrills and spills of Six Day Cycle Races, shown here.

History-making

The Preston North End goalkeeper, Holdcroft, punches clear from Huddersfield Town's centre-forward, McFadyen in the history-making 1938 final at Wembley. The keenly-contested match went into extra time with the score 0 - 0 and ended sensationally, as shown in the second picture.

The historic penalty

Mutch of Preston North End has been fouled in the last goal-less seconds of extra-time in the 1938 final. He has put the ball on the penalty spot and fired it into the Huddersfield net, as shown in our picture, at the very moment the referee blows for time. The Lillywhites therefore become the first-ever finalists to win by a penalty.

War-time international

Len Goulden scores England's third goal in a fine victory over Scotland at Wembley in October, 1944. This international, like most in war-time, was for charity, and attendances were restricted. No caps were awarded and matches did not count as full internationals. As in the First World War, the Football League competition had been abandoned from September, 1939, and there were no Wembley Cup Finals until 1946.

1940's

Peace again at Wembley

This was the happy scene at the first post-war Wembley Cup Final, in which Derby County beat Charlton Athletic by four goals to one, after extra time. There had been all too little quality soccer to watch in the six grim years of war. Now Wembley was itself again, after serving as an emergency dispersal centre for refugees and as a charity fund-raising venue in the war years.

'It was like this . . .'

The strong, hard men of Derby County have carried off the first post-war FA Cup at Wembley, and the BBC microphone takes their comments to millions in the moment of victory over Charlton Athletic. The Rams had won through by 4 - 1 after thirty gruelling minutes of extra-time.

Disappointed fans

Soccer fever is back more strongly than ever, with the 1947 final (in which Charlton Athletic beat Burnley 1 - 0, again after extra time) a complete sell-out despite an increase to 99,370 in the crowd permitted to attend. Thousands were turned away from the gates an hour before the match began.

Mind my ribs !

England's Neil Franklin is impeded by Scotland's Jimmy Delaney as he pounces on a ball that has slipped from Big Frank Swift's grasp in the England penalty area in the first post-war Wembley international between the auld foes, in 1947. The result was a 1 - 1 draw.

New approach to the twin towers

A procession of cars and coaches heads for the opening ceremony of the Olympic Way, the new approach road from the station to the stadium, created in honour of the 1948 Olympic Games. All the facilities of the entire Wembley complex was given over to the XIVth Olympiad.

Rowley nets the second

It is Matt Busby's final in 1948. The dour, delightful Scot has built Manchester United into one of the great post-war sides, and they have little difficulty in beating Blackpool 4 - 2. Their sharpshooting centre-forward, Jack Rowley, is seen here throwing Blackpool's defence into disarray, as he scores United's second goal.

The first authorised 100,000

As the giant scoreboard shows Arsenal 1; Liverpool 0, Compton, Barnes and Mercer of Arsenal combine to take the ball away from Baron of Liverpool in the thrilling 1950 final. Arsenal scored again to win 2 - 0 in one of the finest footballing finals ever seen at Wembley. The crowd reached 100,000 for the first time since 1923, and paid nearly £40,000 for its pleasures.

1950's

Gunners shoot to victory

Liverpool's baggy-shorted goalkeeper, Sidlow, clears from the feet of Arsenal's centre-forward Goring, but Arsenal were to run out winners for the third time, with Lewis scoring both goals in a splendid 2 - 0 victory.

Mercer the magnificent

Arsenal captain, Joe Mercer is chaired by team-mates after the Gunner's third great win at Wembley, in 1950. Front-right is wee Jimmy Logie, and others in the picture are Barnes, Swindin, Scott, Forbes and L. Compton (the last-named incredibly aged 38, and about to make his debut for England at centre-half — the oldest ever to do so).

Jackie Milburn's final

Challenged by Mudie of Blackpool, Newcastle's Jack Milburn swerves and lashes the ball into the net, with his incredible left foot, to produce one of the greatest goals ever seen at Wembley Stadium. It was four o'clock on a Saturday afternoon in April, 1951, and it is still raved about by Tynesiders. The 'Jackie Milburn final' was won by Newcastle United by 2 - 0 before 100,000 fans, most of them from the north.

The Stanley Matthews final

It is Coronation Year (1953) and a radiant Queen Elizabeth II presents to Stanley Matthews the cup winner's medal he had so long sought. The Mighty Maestro, soon to be knighted for his brilliant soccer achievements, had played a principal part in Blackpool's will-they, won't-they victory over Bolton Wanderers by four goals to three.

England bites the turf

Billy Wright leads the England team to defeat on their home turf for the first time ever in 45 years of official internationals against foreign countries. The team nearer the camera is the Mighty Magyers of Hungary, led by their famous captain, Puskas. They slammed in six goals to England's two, in ninety minutes of brilliant play which had the crowd gasping and which would demand a complete re-thinking of England's style and attitudes. Playing at right back for England, on this infamous occasion, was a young man, Alf Ramsay by name.

The old men win

Humbled by Hungary the previous season, the English team, still led by Billy Wright (seen here with Herkenrath, the German captain) made some amends on 1 December 1954 by defeating the World Champions, West Germany, by three goals to one. But it was no pointer for the future. England was saved by her old men of soccer and in particular by the 'clown prince', Len Shackleton, brought back to international honours at 33. Aiding him was Stanley Matthews, whose first appearance against Germany had been in 1938 in Berlin, when England had won 6 - 3. More than 8,000 Germans who had come to Wembley to see England thrashed at home for the second time ever, went home nonplussed. Hungary had beaten England and Germany had beaten Hungary (in the World Cup Final) and yet here were the old men of England beating the young braves of Germany. It just did not make sense.

World Champions bite the turf

German goalkeeper, Fritz Herkenrath, dives full length to save a shot from the great Tom Finney, England's outside-left, in the Wembley international in December, 1954, which England won splendidly by three goals to one. It was the year West Germany had beaten the favoured Hungarians in the Final of the World Cup in tough no-nonsense fashion. The England team now belatedly showed that they, too, could tackle and attack when faced with a strong, hard team.

The Revie Plan

The flags fly at Wembley, as captains R. Paul (Manchester City) and J. Scoular (Newcastle United) grimly lead their teams out for a northern battle royal in the May, 1955 Cup Final. Newcastle were back on the emerald turf for the third time in four years, but City were confident that the Revie Plan (as their deep-lying centre-forward game was becoming known) would give them victory.

Milburn again

'Wor' Jackie Milburn again stars at Wembley when he scores the fastest goal ever in a final, just 45 seconds after kick-off. He is seen here heading the ball in from the first corner of the match to score historically in the course of Newcastle's 3 - 1 victory over Manchester City.

Played with broken neck

This is the moment when Bert Trautmann's neck was accidentally broken in the 1956 Cup Final at Wembley. The German-born goalkeeper had made a number of spectacular saves during Manchester City's 3 - 1 victory over Birmingham City . . . not least this one when he dived at the feet of inside-left Murphy. Drunkenly, Trautmann played on for the remaining 12 minutes of the match, of which he would remember nothing. Although no-one knew how bad his injury was, the crowd, sensing his bravery, cheered him off with a chorus of 'For he's a jolly good fellow'.

Smartness scores

Splendid in their new track-suits, the Nottingham Forest team, here being greeted by the Dukes of Edinburgh and Gloucester, went on to thrash Luton Town by 2 - 1 in the 1959 final.

Frozen in action

Unlucky Scotland just fail to equalise against England, at Wembley in 1959, when Scottish centre-forward Herd lashes in a tremendous shot, with Hopkinson, the England goalkeeper, well beaten. Alas, the ball accidentally hits Leggat, the Scotland outside-right and bounces clear. England win this one by the only goal of the match.

Eng-land, Eng-land

Jimmy Armfield, England's right back, tussles for the ball with Portugal's great inside-right F. Eusebio (8) in the World Cup Match at Wembley, which Englana splendidly won by two goals to nil on 25 October, 1961.

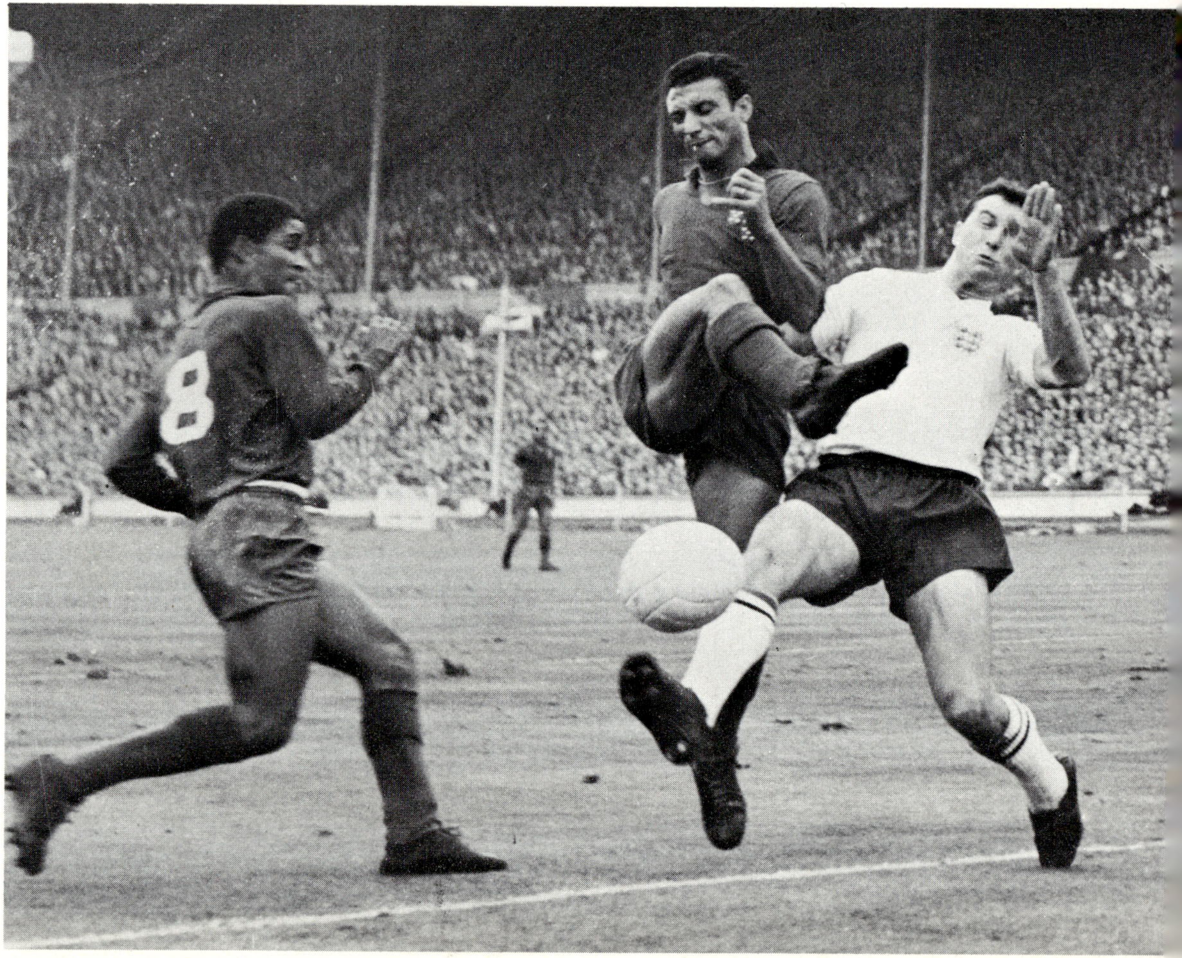

Amateurs at Wembley

The Football Association's Amateur Challenge Cup is now also drawing ever-increasing crowds to Wembley. Here, in 1961, R. Graves, Walthamstow Avenue's outside right puts the ball past B. Bowmaker, the West Auckland Town's goalkeeper, to score Avenue's first goal, in their 2 - 1 victory. Attendance was a record 45,000 and receipts were £16,212.

Twice in a row

This is the powerful Tottenham Hotspur team that won the FA Cup for the second time in a row in 1962, when they beat Burnley by three goals to one before 100,000 people, who had paid a record £53,837 to see the match. This final unusually featured a penalty, from which Blanchflower scored for Spurs in the last ten minutes of the match. But it was all over by then, anyway. The great Spurs team was: Brown; Baker, Henry; Blanchflower, Norman, Mackay; Medwin, White, Smith, Greaves and Jones.

Taking a risk

It's Amateur Cup day again at Wembley (1962). In spectacular fashion, P. Rhodes, the Hounslow Town goalkeeper just manages to deflect a shot from the feet of A. Coates, Crook Town's centre forward. Crook Town would win out by 4 - 0 in a replay at Middlesborough, the Wembley match having ended in a 1 - 1 draw. It would be the fourth time they would take home the coveted trophy for which as many as 370 clubs compete.

Only the fifth

The ball has been deflected over the bar and the England players watch its flight, but Millington, the acrobatic Wales goalkeeper is still in the air looking backwards to be sure that Hill's shot has not gone into the net. It was the 73rd home international between the two countries, but only the fifth to be played at Wembley.

On the spot

It's a penalty in the England-Austria game in 1962, and left-half Ron Flowers has made no mistake, with goalkeeper Fraydl beaten all the way. This was the second goal in a fine match which England won convincingly by three goals to one.

The two Matts

The Cup Final teams of 1963 take the field at Wembley, led by their managers, Matt Gillies (Leicester City) and Matt Busby (Manchester United). Somehow, despite the worst weather in the history of soccer, the Cup programme had been completed in time for the final to be held on Saturday, 25 May. A fantastic £88,882 was paid by the 100,000 spectators, an increase of more than 100 per cent in 10 years. But still the ticket applications were over-subscribed many, many times over.

United again win the Cup

Leicester City's international goalkeeper, Gordon Banks (believed by many to be the greatest in the world) bites the Wembley turf in May, 1963, as he watches centre-forward D. Herd's shot whip past him into the net for Manchester United's second goal. Busby's rebuilt United were to run out worthy winners by three goals to one.

The Pools

It's the awful winter of 1962-3 (when in all over 400 games had to be rearranged because of the weather) and with most fixtures called off on Saturday, 26 January, the Football Pools' Selection Board has to meet to decide what the results would have been if the matches had been played. The serious and dedicated 'veterans' chosen for the job are (l. to r.) Ted Drake, Arthur Ellis, Tom Finney, Tommy Lawton and George Young. At this point the Football League was receiving something like £250,000 a year from the Pools for the use of fixture lists and, from 1964, a new agreement would guarantee to the Football League and Scottish League a total minimum of £500,000 a year.

High-jumper

Built like men and playing a highly-skilled, almost professional game, these are schoolboys having their annual moment of glory at Wembley. It is April, 1963, and England outside-left J. Husband jumps high to head the ball away from S. Derrett, the Wales right-back.

Cooper v. Clay

Boxing came and went at Wembley, as the directors blew hot and cold on its possibilities as a crowd-puller. But few will dispute that the first post-war bout there — between Henry Cooper and Cassius Clay in June, 1963 — was one of the greatest ever seen in Britain. Held outdoors in the stadium, it did not attract as big a crowd as had been hoped, as can be seen in this picture.

Contrast in black and white

Bloody but game, Henry Cooper ducks to avoid a left from Cassius Clay in the course of an honourable defeat in which he was the first man to have the champion on the canvas . . . at Wembley, in June, 1963.

Game to the last

His eye cut and puffed, Cooper gallantly fights back against Clay at Wembley Stadium on a June night in 1963.

Raising the roof

This is the famous and infamous new roof at Wembley seen during the England-Uruguay match on 6 May, 1964, which the home side won by two goals to one. On the plus side, the reconstructed stadium now afforded complete protection from the weather to all the 100,000 crowd. But on the minus side, the £500,000 roof was to be blamed for the deterioration of the famous turf.

Hammers at their best

It is 1964, and England's preparation for the 1966 World Cup is beginning to get under way. Three of Alf Ramsay's greatest prospects — Bobby Moore, Martin Peters and Geoff Hurst — are seen in fabulous action at Wembley when West Ham United convincingly defeat Preston North End 3 - 2 to win the FA Cup for the first time in its 65-year history. Our picture shows J. Sissons scoring West Ham's first goal.

Hammers triumphant

In the memorable European Cup Winners' Cup Final at Wembley on 19 May, 1965, the capacity crowd thrills to see West Ham United defeat Munich 1860 by two goals to nil, there having been no score at half-time. In our picture, Jim Standen is seen making a characteristically brave save from Munich's inside-left, P. Grosser. The history-making Hammers' team read: Standen; Kirkup, Burkett; Peters, Brown, Moore; Sealey, Boyce, Hurst, Dear, and Sissons. Munich 1860, a physically strong, intelligent, thrusting side were frequently thwarted by Standen's fine goalkeeping. West Ham, who had lost Johnny Byrne through injury, nevertheless put up a splendid performance and were worthy winners.

The too-late tackle

The Rugby League Cup Final, introduced to Wembley by Arthur Elvin, has over the years defied all predictions that it should be staged in the north, where it has its home. Year after year the stadium is packed with fans who enjoy the trip to London as a high-spot of their year. In this spectacular shot, taken during the 1965 final between Wigan and Hunslet, Trevor Lake of Wigan is seen scoring the winning try.

Pain and victory

With the World Cup series approaching. Alf Ramsey has been experimenting with various systems, including 4 - 2 - 4 and 4 - 3 - 3 combinations, in his search for the best style for an all-new England team. In May, 1965, hopes ran high when Hungary was defeated at Wembley by the only goal in the game — scored by Jimmy Greaves — but on the whole it was a season of indifferent international performances. In our picture, Hungary goal-keeper J. Gelei snatches the ball from the feet of outside-right Terry Paine (last-minute replacement for Bobby Charlton) as Hungary skipper and left-half Sipos attempts to assist.

Everything on ice

Ice spectaculars and pantomimes had long been a feature of winter seasons at the Empire Pool, Wembley. Typical of them is this Tom Arnold version of the Disney classic, ***Snow White and the Seven Dwarfs,*** staged in 1965. The show, featuring an international cast of over 150, ran for three months, from Boxing Day, and broke all previous records. Our picture shows Carole Anne, as Snow White, high-kicking over the heads of her dwarfs.

Good-humoured British bobbies

Millions of television viewers enjoyed the chase which resulted after several minutes of hilarious Keystone Cops comedy, in the eventual capture and removal of this Everton fan in the 1966 final in which his club triumphed over Sheffield Wednesday by 3 - 2. For the first time, the crowd paid over £100,000 for the privilege of watching a fine game.

Unbeatable England

When Geoff Hurst shoots a ball from close in, there are very few goalkeepers in the world who can stop it. Certainly, Wales goalie, Millington cannot, as the super-England team of 1966 crushed his team by five goals to one.

On top of the world

The Jules Rimet World Cup Trophy is held aloft by England captain, Bobby Moore, as his victorious 1966 world-beaters jog-trot around Wembley Stadium to the rapturous, almost unbelieving cheers of the huge crowd. For England to win in her own stadium before her own crowd (plus the largest world television audience ever recorded, reckoned to be in excess of 400 million) was almost too much. The gold trophy, insured for £30,000, was worth a million and more at that moment to the brilliant young lads of Sir Alf Ramsey's well-schooled team, which had won its way through the net of 53 participating countries. England's immortal line-up in the final at Wembley was: Banks; Cohen, Wilson; Stiles, Charlton (J.), Moore; Ball, Hurst, Hunt, Charlton (R.) and Peters. The result, after extra time, was England 4, West Germany 2. It was like winning a world war again, only sweeter.

Glory, glory, hallelujah !

Roger Hunt, England's spearhead of attack and himself a leading goalscorer in the series, leaps in the air in delight as Geoff Hurst scores the first of his three great goals in the 1966 final — the first-ever hat-trick in a World Cup Final.

It's there !

With England in the lead by 2 - 1, and only seconds to go, the vast Wembley crowd prepares to raise the new roof of the stadium. But it is not to be. This is Germany's second goal which forced extra time. Wolfgang Weber (white shirt on ground, left) has stabbed at the ball in the crowded goal mouth, and it has shot past Ray Wilson (seated) and Gordon Banks (recumbent). Weber shouts his joy. Uwe Seeler (behind him) can scarcely believe it. Karl Schnellinger raises his arms in salute, and Bobby Moore does likewise in protest. A grim Jackie Charlton runs towards the goal-line, just too late, as George Cohen prays.

Peters rises to the occasion

Rugged Martin Peters goes in to tackle Lothar Emmerich, with Cohen in support, in the course of England's great victory over West Germany in the World Cup Final at Wembley in 1966. Peters was brilliant on the day — better than he had ever been for his club; invaluable in defence as well as in attack. He it was who 'made' several of England's goals, on her way to victory, with his curving, hanging passes to the centre. Cohen, too, rose to the height of his powers on the great day — a sure stalwart in England's hard-working defence in the punishing two hours of play.

This was the one !

The ball bounces from the cross-bar towards the line, as 22 players and 100,000 fans hold their breath. This was England's controversial third goal, which is still argued about in Germany to this day. Geoff Hurst (not in the picture) has shot brilliantly, and Roger Hunt prepares to signal the winner, as goalkeeper Hans Tilkowski is clearly beaten. But the rebound of the ball is so fast no-one in the crowd can be absolutely certain that it fell beyond the line. The referee, after consulting the Russian linesman, awarded the goal and pandemonium ensued among the German fans. But subsequent examination of film, tape and still pictures cleared the matter up for all fair-minded aficionados. It was a goal. It was also the goal that mattered. England were the greatest.

Bonetti beaten

It's a goal. Jimmy Greaves and Terry Venables signal their delight, as Robertson (not in picture) beats Bonetti to score Tottenham Hotspur's first goal against Chelsea in the 1967 final.

Jennings saves

Acrobatic as a cat, Jennings the Spurs' goalkeeper pushes the ball over the top from a powerful Hateley header in the 1967 all-London Cup Final in which Tottenham Hotspur were worthy winners over Chelsea by two goals to one.

The real Mackay

The incomparable Dave Mackay, having fought his way back to fitness after breaking his left leg twice in ten months, holds the FA Cup triumphantly aloft, after leading Spurs to victory at Wembley, in 1967, against Chelsea. In doing so, Mackay became the most honoured player in soccer history — the only one ever to have earned Scottish FA Cup-winners' and FA Cup-winner's medals in addition to many other international and club successes. The scenes in Tottenham as the team, the captain and the cup arrived at the Town Hall atop a double-decker bus will long be remembered in the borough.

A win for QPR

It's the Football League Cup at Wembley, in 1967, and Queens Park Rangers are attacking the West Bromwich Albion goal. Rodney Marsh has just missed with a header and his captain, Mike Keen has pounced on the rebound. Alas, with WBA goalie R. Shepherd well beaten, Kean's shot hits the post; nevertheless Rangers win the day by 3 - 2.

Eng-land win again

The spirit of the World Cup lived on at Wembley on 24 May, 1967 when England showed complete dominance over the European Nations' Cup holders, Spain. In our picture, the great attacking trio of Mullery, Hurst and Greaves are stopped only by the flying fist of Spain's goal-keeper, Jose Iribar. England won the match 2 - 0.

A fine amateur match

Unusually, the FA Amateur Cup Final at Wembley ends in a no-score draw after extra time. In a moment that could have brought victory to Enfield, centre-forward R. Hill heads towards the Skelmersdale United net, with goalkeeper T. Crosbie beaten all the way, but a United defender clears the ball before it crosses the line. In the replay, at Maine Road, Manchester, however, Enfield made no mistake in a positive 3 - 0 win, with Hill this time scoring twice. This fine match drew 75,000 to Wembley and 55,388 to Maine Road.

Height helps

'Hold on there and give me a chance', Roger Hunt (England) seems to be saying to Harvey (Ireland) in a tussle for the ball in the Wembley international which ended in a 2 - 0 victory for England in November, 1967.

Scotland beats World Champions

Scotland collides with England (in the recumbent shapes of Gordon Banks and Dennis Law) at Wembley, in April, 1967. The collision between the two teams also produced the surprise result of the year, with Scotland beating the Auld Enemy convincingly by 3 - 2.

Blow football

Geoff Hurst puffs out his cheeks as if to blow the ball into the net in a second half raid by England on the Scottish goal, with Simpson defeated and Bobby Charlton ready to follow through. Nevertheless the World Cup winners went down to Scotland, on England's national turf, by three goals to two.

Scotland 3: England 2

Goal no. 2 for Scotland, in April, 1967, is beautifully contrived by Bobby Lennox, with Gordon Banks diving too late and Bobby Moore (left) unable to help. Wembley has been turned into Bannockburn for the day, with Scotland 3 - 2 victors over the World Champs.

Snow on their boots

In an exciting 2 - 2 draw, England met Russia at Wembley in the snow of December, 1967. As Russian goalkeeper, Y. Psenitchnikov, lies helpless on the frozen turf, Alan Ball swerves away triumphantly from scoring England's first goal.

Ballet in the snow

Like ballet-dancers, three figures rise into the air under the floodlights of Wembley Stadium. Geoff Hurst heads the ball past the Russian goalkeeper, of the unpronouncable name, while centre-half Anithkin tries to get in on the act. The final score was 2 - 2.

Peacocks rampant

Leeds United captain Billy Bremner holds aloft the League Cup after his team's fine 1 - 0 victory over Arsenal in March, 1968. Chairing their Scottish international skipper are Gary Sprake and Jackie Charlton.

Extra time again

West Bromwich Albion, led by their captain, G. Williams, show the FA Cup to the crowd after the presentation at Wembley. It was the fifth time the club had won the most coveted of trophies. They had also won the League Cup in 1966 and had been runners-up in 1967. This time they had conquered the mighty Everton by 1 - 0 after extra time.

Cutting up rough

The Royal International Horse Show is held on the sacred turf of Wembley in July, 1968 for the first time. The subsequent cutting up of the emerald turves by the horses' hooves is blamed for the bad condition of the playing surface in 1969.

Cuddles in the rain

Boots sink into the mud, and surface water sprays the players, as a Leeds' attacker falls under the bodies of two Wakefield Trinity defenders in the Rugby League Cup Final at Wembley in May, 1968.

The young Royals

Continuing the Royal tradition that had been begun by King George V and Queen Mary at Wembley, in 1923, Princess Anne meets the teams at the 1969 Cup Final between Leicester City and Manchester City. In our picture the Princess is presented to the Leicester team by their 21-year-old captain, D. Nish.

Count the goalkeepers

There seem to be more Blues' shirts around their goal than raindrops at a Manchester wedding, as A. Lochhead (Leicester City's centre-forward) puts one over the bar in the 1969 Cup Final, won by Manchester City by one goal to nil.

The cabbage patch match

The fabulous Joe Mercer, Manchester City manager, and himself a cup winner, takes his turn at showing the FA Cup to the fans after the Blues' fine victory, in trying conditions, over Leicester City by 1 - 0. Mercer had described the pitch before the game began as 'a cabbage patch.' But his fine team, not least Francis Lee and Colin Bell (shown here with their boss) had triumphed nonetheless. Despite the mud, 100,000 fans had considered it worth paying a record £128,238 to watch the match and no-one could have gone home disappointed with the value given by the well-matched teams.

The Cup has gone to his head

Tony Book, the triumphant Manchester City captain, shows the crowd what the best footballers are wearing this year . . . any year.

Poacher triumphs

Showing once more the greatest poacher's leap in football, Jackie Charlton soars to head the ball, from a corner, firmly past Portugal's goalkeeper, Henrique, to score England's only goal in their victory over their oldest ally, in December, 1969.

Amateur triumph

North Shields' team members chair their young captain, R. Tatum, as he holds the FA Amateur cup aloft after defeating Sutton United 2 - 1 in April, 1969.

Not so funny

Princess Margaret shares a joke with Arsenal's Bobby Gould before the League Cup Final, in which they unexpectedly went down to Swindon Town, by 3 - 1, in March, 1969.

Crowd behaviour

The League Cup Final of 1969 was marred by fighting in the terraces before and during the match. But the British bobby triumphed as always. This young fan is removed from the crowd by constables little older than he is.

Vive la France

It's coming up to World Cup year again and England captain Bobby Moore looks suitably serious, as he exchanges pennants with France's captain Bernard Bosquier before the international match at Wembley in March, 1969. England triumphed to the tune of five goals to nil.

First blood to Chelsea

Houseman scores Chelsea's first goal, as the muddy ball slips through Sprake's hands in the sensational 1970 Wembley FA Cup Final.

1970's

Blast it!

Garry Sprake of Leeds has allowed Chelsea to score in the 1970 FA Cup Final at Wembley, and he shows his displeasure in uncharacteristically emotional fashion.

Stockings down and calves cramped

Inevitably cramp became a killer for the participants in the extra-time played in the historic Leeds Chelsea Cup Final of 1970. In our picture, Chelsea's McCready gets a helping hand from team-mate Hutchinson as he collapses with cramp at the end of the incredibly hard-fought match, which Chelsea eventually won (for the first time ever) in the replay.

Arabesque in the mud

Chelsea's Ian Hutchinson (10) and Norman Hunter (6) of Leeds are caught in a dancing pattern of limbs in the Wembley mud in the sensational FA Cup Final of 1970, leading to the first replay at that stage for fifty years.

The quagmire final

Mike Doyle of Manchester City beats West Bromwich Albion 'keeper, John Osborne, in the mud and the Blues win the 1970 League Cup to set up a recent record which brings pride to Maine Road, taking in: 1965-66, Champions, division two; 1967-1968, Champions, division one; 1968-69, Winners of FA Cup . . . and which puts them into the same sort of class as the great Arsenal side of the 'thirties.

A facelift for the stadium

The much-maligned-of-late playing surface at the Empire Stadium, Wembley, is completely re-turfed over a period of eight weeks, in the summer of 1970, to restore it to its once-hallowed state, in good time for the 50th birthday celebrations. In the process, extensive drainage and reconstruction work is carried out under the supervision of the Turf Research Institute, the ground being excavated to a depth of about 18 inches. The new turves have been acquired from the practice course at Ganton Golf Club, near Scarborough, Yorkshire, and the cost of the operation fell little short of £35,000.

BISHOP

HAVERING
HAVERING

We did it!

Martin Chivers and his captain, Alan Mullery, flank their manager, Bill Nicholson, as they hold aloft the League Cup, which Tottenham Hotspur have won in 1971 by 2 - 0 over a brave but outclassed-on-the-day Aston Villa.

Villa get the Chivers

White-shirted Martin Chivers scores his side's first goal in the Wembley final of the 1971 League Cup competition, as an Aston Villa player appears to clutch him from behind. Chivers scored both goals in the Spurs' 2 - 0 victory over Villa.

Bonanza Bonus

On 8th May, 1971, Wembley Stadium echoed to the biggest roar since the World Cup final of 1966. Arsenal had beaten Liverpool 2 - 1 in extra-time to become only the second club in the almost 50 year existence of Wembley to win the League Championship and the FA Cup in the same season. It was only the fourth such coup in the history of the game—the second by a London club, Tottenham Hotspur having gained the distinction in 1960-61 . . . following Aston Villa in 1896-97 and Preston in 1898-99.

Frank McLintock, Arsenal Captain and Footballer of the Year holds the treasured trophy aloft, chaired by his weary but triumphant Arsenal team-mates, each of whom could be about £12,000 richer by way of a bonanza bonus for achieving the delectable double.

Heading High

This was the goal that nearly was . . . that should have been . . . that ought to have sewn up the game for the Gunners in normal time. It was the last minute of the first half. George Armstrong had run into the correct position to accept an opportunist cross from the right. But, instead of heading low, he headed high into Liverpool goalkeeper, Ray Clemence's instinctive clutch, Frank McLintock, rated by some Arsenal's greatest skipper (despite strong claims from supporters of such as Alex James, Joe Mercer and Eddie Hapgood) looks on (centre) almost unbelieving that the chance has been missed.

The Kop

Even the Kop cheered Arsenal's victory double in May, 1971, as they paid tribute in sporting fashion to worthy rivals and vowed to be back at Wembley soon . . . as winners. Both sides had given everything for 120 minutes under punishing conditions. In extra-time defensive tactics had been set aside in favour of attacking play Liverpool had acquitted themselves courageously throughout, but Arsenal had won through with disciplined team spirit and a bit of luck.

LIVERPOOL
F C

Liverpool Breaks

It's the equaliser, George Graham, perhaps the best footballer of the 22 in the final, and later to be voted player of the match, scores the goal that brought Arsenal right back into the game (at 1 - 1) and which paved the way for their fantastic 'double'. It was a somewhat scrambled, if well-deserved goal, and the slow-motion television films seemed to show that Kelly, rather than Graham sent the ball into the net. But the fact was that Arsenal had at last broken through the best defence in soccer and had the strength to do it again a few minutes later for victory. Kelly, in the end, was credited.

This Way Up

Steve Heighway, who brilliantly scored Liverpool's only goal and brought the crucial 1971 final to life, is outsmarted for once by Arsenal's Simpson, who clears by means of an acrobatic scizzors kick. In the main, Heighway played his usual high-stepping, prancing, dribbling game - as unpredictable as it was traditional in its skills - and gave his many fans the usual value for money. There will undoubtedly be a Cup Winner's medal for the Liverpool 'egghead' in the years to come. This year the Gunners had frustrated him by keeping their sights unwaveringly trained on the ultimate target of the soccer double - the Cup and the League.

Crowned

His shirt soaked in sweat, Charlie George, of the flowing locks and twinkling feet, is deservedly crowned after the great Gunners' victory in the 1971 FA Cup Final at Wembley. George, the star midfield player and the young hero to most Arsenal fans, appropriately scored the winning goal in the extra-time 2 - 1 victory.

The Million Pound Stadium

1971 generally was the year when Wembley struck it richer than rich. By the end of the season, receipts from 11 major matches reached around £1 million pounds for the first time.

The Arsenal-Liverpool Final grossed the highest amount ever, when receipts topped £187,000 (which had only ever been beaten by the £204,000 'take' from the World Cup final in 1966).

The minimum admission charge had been raised in 1971 to £1, and the top price to £5. Even so, £4 tickets were changing hands outside the ground for £60. Programme sales brought in a record £32,000. A catering staff of 500 provided 25,000 sandwiches, 20,000 cups of tea, 60,000 bottles of beer and 500 bottles of whisky for the 100,000 fans. Outside the giant stadium, 50 car park officials had to deal with 5,000 cars and 500 coaches. And, when it was all over, 20 tons of rubbish had to be cleared from the stands.

It was a long cry from the White Horse final of 1923, but Wembley's great spirit as the true home of soccer lives on undimmed as it approaches the kick-off for its second half century . . .